Granny Trish

The Stories
of
Jack and Rory

Original story by Patricia Mackie
Edited by Emily Marcham
Book cover and illustrations by Quynh Rua
Published by Oldbird Publishing
www.oldbirdpublishing.com

To all my Grandchildren

xxx

Table of contents

PROLOGUE

Hi! I'm Frankie! If you're lucky enough to have a granny like my Granny Trish, then you're very lucky indeed. Granny Trish makes the best biscuits to dunk in your hot chocolate and she tells the best stories too! Every time we go over to her house to visit, all of the grandchildren (even the big ones) want Granny Trish to tell us a story before bed. Today is no different, and I've asked Granny Trish to tell us my most favourite story collection of all, about two Labradors called Jack and Rory.

Oh, one more thing... Granny Trish always forgets when she's telling stories that you have to start by saying 'once upon a time', so I'll say that now for her – otherwise, we'll have to begin all over again!

Once upon a time...

Story 1:
PERKINS

It was a very cold and frosty January morning, with thick, white snow covering the farm courtyard. The farm was near the small village of St Cyrus, on the northeast coast of Scotland.

Perkins the Labrador puppy shivered and snuggled closer to his mummy, brothers, and sisters, trying to get warm. It was soooo cold in the kennel! The concrete floor wasn't heated, and Perkins was only eight weeks old.

Although Perkins didn't know it yet, today was going to be a special day. Today, he was going to meet his new family and go to live in his new home – a warm, cosy house where he'd have a lovely, fleecy blanket and comfy bed all to himself.

The farmer's wife came bustling out of the farmhouse and opened the kennel, filling Perkins' dishes with some dried food and water before going back inside. He quickly jumped up and excitedly scoffed everything down, barely pausing to chew.

When he had finished, he happily licked his paws, lips, and full tummy. Then, he trotted around the enclosed yard outside the kennel, watching in fascination as the snow fell. The white of the snow looked even brighter against Perkins' silky, black fur.

Not long after, the farmhouse kitchen door opened again, and out came the farmer and his wife. They walked towards a car that was slowly driving down the farm road. When it stopped, three people got out and spoke to the farmer, who turned and pointed to Parsnip, Perkins' brother. The family approached the yard, crouching down to look at Parsnip, but he was afraid and scurried back inside the kennel to hide behind Mummy. Perkins wasn't afraid though, he was curious. *Who were these people, and why were they looking at them?* he wondered, tilting his head to the side as he pondered.

The little boy, whose name was Finn, put his hand through the netting of the yard and Perkins slowly walked over to cautiously sniff the boy's fingers. Having decided he liked the boy, he happily licked Finn's hand and wagged his tail as the boy stroked his head. The boy's mum and dad spoke to him and pointed to Parsnip who had peeked out from behind Mummy, but Finn shook his head and pointed to Perkins.

Seeing this, the farmer walked over and said very kindly to the boy, 'Laddie, Parsnip would be a better choice for you. Perkins is a bit boisterous and not so easy for a family.'

Finn's eyes filled with tears, and he looked towards his mum and dad, 'I really want Perkins. I can tell he likes me; he came to sniff my hand and he let me stroke him. Please, please, can we have him, pleeeease?' he begged.

Finn's mum and dad looked at each other, then they looked at the farmer, who shrugged his shoulders and pulled a 'have it your own way' sort of face. With a resigned sigh, the farmer un-latched the door of the kennel, picked up Perkins, and put the puppy in Finn's arms. Finn's eyes lit up as he looked up at the farmer and promised, 'I will always look after Perkins. He is the best present I have ever had! I'll love him, walk him, take care of him, make sure he is happy, and never ever hungry. Thank you so much!'

The farmer chuckled warmly as he reached out and ruffled Finn's hair, 'I believe you will look after Perkins, son. I hope you have a great life together.'

The family climbed into the car and Finn sat in the back with Perkins on his lap, wrapped in a cosy blanket. Perkins was look-ing around him wondering where on earth he was going as they drove away, the farmhouse slowly disappearing from his sight.

Story 2:
THE FAMILY

On the journey home, Perkins, who had never been in a car before or away from his mummy, began to feel a bit strange. He wanted to play with his brothers and sisters and feel the warmth of Mummy licking his fur. Without Mummy, who would teach him how to grow into a proper, well-behaved Labrador? Plus, he didn't know if he liked the noise of this strange contraption he had been taken into. It moved too quickly which made his tummy turn over.

After what felt like forever to Perkins, the car finally stopped. Finn carried Perkins into his new home and placed the puppy down on the floor. His curiosity was piqued. So, overcoming his fear, Perkins wandered around the kitchen, sniffing here, there, and everywhere. His nose was twitching at the dozens of strange and different smells in this new room. It felt nice and warm here too. Finn scooped up Perkins and took him over to a basket that had a furry lining and a soft blanket inside with little paws printed all over it. Perkins put one paw in with trepidation; it felt very comfy so he put another paw in, then all four paws, before turning round and round to find the perfect position. Finally, having decided that, *yes, this is the one,* he lay down, yawned, and promptly fell asleep.

When he woke up, there seemed to be lots and lots of eyes staring down at him. *Woof, woof, woof!* he barked, panicking. He couldn't see Finn, where was he? He liked Finn and his smell made him feel safe. He missed Mummy.

Through the bodies, Finn appeared. Finn picked Perkins up and let him smell his brothers one by one. It turned out that all the faces were just Finn's five older brothers who were all eager to meet the new puppy.

'What's he called?' said one of them.

Finn looked a bit sheepish and said with raised eyes, 'Perkins!'

'Perkins!' they all chorused, 'what sort of name is that?'

'Oh no, we don't like that name. He'll have to be called something else,' said one of the brothers.

Perkins listened with interest, he didn't really mind his name. All of his litter had names that began with the letter 'P' and they quite liked their matching names. However, the boys definitely did not seem to like the name Perkins and were now busy discussing a new one for him.

All sorts of names were thrown into the mix as the boys excitedly called names over each other:

'Buzz!'

'No, Freddie'

'What about Blackie, after his fur?'

'Hamish!'

'What? No way!'

'Harvey?'

'Marley?'

'No! He doesn't look like a Marley!'

Hmm, the boys were stumped. None of the names were right. Nothing seemed to suit the puppy. The kitchen door opened and Jenny, the boys' mum, came into the room. 'Ah, I hear you are all trying to come up with a new name for Perkins. What about Jack? It was my dad's name and he was a wonderful person. It would remind me of Dad whenever someone shouted his name,' she said with a smile. The boys all stopped talking and thought about the name their mum had suggested. They huddled together and whispered conspiringly. Finally, a decision was made. They all looked up and Finn announced, 'Ok Mum, we all agree. Jack is his name.'

And that's how Perkins became Jack.

Story 3:
SETTLING IN

Jack became used to his new name, his new home in Kirkcaldy, and his new family who all loved him, very quickly. He still thought about Mummy and his brothers and sisters, but because he was never really on his own, and there was always someone around to stroke and cuddle him, feed him, or play with him, he didn't miss them too badly. There was only one thing missing in his new home: When would he be taken out for a walk? He wasn't sure what a walk *was* exactly, but Finn was always talking about the 'W' word and it sounded very fun indeed. But, so far, the infamous walk had not happened.

He had been with his new family for two weeks when one day, Matt, the boys' dad, picked Jack up from his cosy bed and said, 'Well, my boy, we're off to visit the vet for your second injection.'

Jack had been given the first injection at eight weeks when he lived with the farmer and his wife. Today, he was due to get the next one.

Matt and Jack arrived at the vet's clinic for their appointment. They were taken into a room and a man (the vet) and his nurse took Jack from Matt. They popped him onto the examining table and checked him all over before finally giving him his injection. This would protect Jack from illnesses that can be very dangerous for puppies. The vet also gave him a tablet in case he had picked up a thing called worms when he was with his mummy at the farm.

Matt asked when Jack could go for his first walk and the vet said he would still have to wait for twelve whole days!

On the twelfth day, there was great excitement in the house. Who would get to take Jack for his first walk? They all wanted to be the first one. Eventually, it was decided that Finn, Matt, and Jenny would be the ones to take him because they had chosen him and he was Finn's dog really as he was a tenth birthday present.

Jack already had a very posh, shiny, red collar, and now he had a matching lead that clipped onto it. Jack wasn't sure if he liked the lead as it stopped him from being able to run too far. But it was important to keep him safe when he was walking on the pavement and it stopped him from running into the road.

Out of the gate they went, and *wow!* There were lots and lots of new smells he had never smelt before. This was exciting! Jack strained against his lead trying to sniff everything he could. Suddenly, he stopped in his tracks. Wait, what was this coming towards him? It was very big, with curly brown fur and it was wagging its tail. Another dog!

When they came face-to-face, Finn's mum and dad stopped to speak to the man walking the very friendly, very waggy-tailed, very large Labradoodle, who sniffed and walked around a confused Jack at least six times before deciding Jack wasn't all that interesting. The Labradoodle pulled his lead to let his owner know he wanted to get on with his walk.

Soon they arrived at the park which had even more interesting smells and soft grass to run on. Jack was having so much fun he didn't want the walk to end! But Matt picked him up after only a short walk because puppies aren't allowed long walks until their legs and hips are strong enough. So, off they went back home. After all of the excitement Jack suddenly felt very tired indeed. *Time for a snooze*, he thought, climbing into his comfy bed.

Story 4:

RORY

Jack was very happy in his new home, life was brilliant! He loved Finn, the boys, Jenny, and Matt. Walking with the family and meeting new friends in the park was the best. He was, however, sometimes quite sad when he had to leave his friends in the park and come home. But, honestly, he knew he was very lucky to live with such a kind and caring family, even though he missed the rough and tumble of his brothers and sisters.

One morning in April, Matt was relaxing with a cup of coffee, reading the weekend newspaper. Folding up his paper, he looked at Jenny and said, 'Stop what you are doing; we're going on a surprise journey today, and I think you're going to like it.'

So, Jack, Finn, Matt, and Jenny piled into the car (the brothers were all out doing various 'things') and set off on their mystery outing.

After driving for a few hours, Matt announced that the next turning was their destination – Blythe Bridge in the Scottish Borders. They drove up into the driveway of a large house and all tumbled out. The huge wooden front door opened and a lady appeared. She smiled and invited them into the house saying, 'Follow me. They're all outside in the garden.'

They? Who was she talking about? *Oh wow!* As they walked around into the garden they saw who she was talking about. There, playing on the grass, were five adorable yellow Labrador puppies! Jenny turned to her husband with a puzzled look on her face. Matt explained that he had seen an advertisement in the paper describing the puppies for sale and that their birthday was the same date as Jenny's, the seventh of February. He couldn't resist the idea of surprising Jenny with a new puppy, and so here they were.

Funnily enough, this wasn't the first pet Jenny had been given as a gift. Years ago, the boys gave Jenny a cat, Domino, as a Christmas gift. Domino mostly ignored Jenny, so hopefully the new puppy wouldn't!

Jenny walked slowly round the grass watching the puppies playing. Suddenly one of them broke away from his brothers and sisters and trotted across to inspect Jenny, who lifted him up and cuddled him, announcing, 'This is the one.'

'Oh,' said the lady, 'that's Fraser. He has a bit of history. A family came to buy him three days ago; they had never had a dog before and lived in a flat in the centre of Edinburgh, two flights up. The first night Fraser was with them he cried all night (as puppies do!), and the next day they brought him back saying they couldn't put up with the noise he was making!'

'Well,' Jenny replied laughing, 'that's their loss and our gain. We certainly won't be bringing him back!'

Jack was curious to see this new face next to him in the car. Finn sat beside them both and informed Jack that this was the newest family member and he would be Jack's new friend and playmate. The two puppies snuggled up together and promptly fell asleep beside Finn. When they arrived home the boys were astonished but delighted to see not one but *two* puppies appearing from the car!

'This is Fraser, our new addition to the family!' said Jenny with a smile.

'FRASER!' chorused the boys, 'what sort of name is that? That's not a dog's name!'

Again, all sorts of names were thrown into the pot, and finally, it was decided Fraser would now be known as Rory, and so began *The Stories of Jack and Rory*.

Aside from Frankie

See, I bet you were super confused when there was only one dog at first and the dogs' names were different to start with. That's why Granny Trish's stories are the best. They always have unexpected parts!

I think the boys in this story were right to change the puppies' names. Jack and Rory sound much better than Perkins and Fraser. What would you call a new puppy if you got one?

Also, I think it's sad that Rory was given back by the first owners; but it was just as well he did, as he ended up with a great family who would never give him back. Granny Trish says you should always think long and hard about getting a pet because 'dogs are for life, not just for Christmas!'

Sorry, I will let Granny Trish carry on with the story now. She always says I shouldn't interrupt, but sometimes I can't help myself!

Story 5:

GETTING TOGETHER

Jack and Rory soon became firm friends. They played together, walked together, ate together, and slept together, which they really loved because they were never alone or felt lonely. Jack was slightly more boisterous and a tad bossy. Rory had a very placid nature but, any time Jack was getting a little bit uppity, Rory would gently tell him off.

One day, when the boys were all at school, Jenny decided to take Jack and Rory to the beach where they could run for miles and have fun in the sea. So off they went, jumping enthusiastically out of the car and running down towards the sea where they had fun running in and out of the water, splashing each other, and racing through the waves. Suddenly, Jack spotted something further out and started swimming frantically towards seven black dots in the distance.

Rory liked being in the water but he wasn't quite such a good swimmer, so he preferred to stay nearer the shore. Meanwhile,

Jenny realised that what Jack had spotted were a mummy duck and her six little ducklings! The mummy duck had now noticed Jack swimming towards her family and so, to divert his attention from them, she paddled off in a different direction. Luckily for the duck family, it worked. But it was not so fortunate for poor Jack, who was now a long way from the shore.

As they stood watching this scene from the beach Jenny and Rory became more and more concerned. All the shouting and barking from them was totally ignored by Jack, who was determined to reach the ducks, and hadn't noticed how far he was from the shore.

Having succeeded in her plan to keep her babies safe from the strange intruder, the mummy duck flew off to join her ducklings, leaving Jack behind. He was now very confused, lost, and frightened. He turned in circles trying to find out where he was but couldn't see anything familiar, and he could no longer see Jenny and Rory. By now, he was so exhausted that he had no strength left to swim. Then, all of a sudden, he was aware of something beside him nudging him along. It was Rory herding him towards the beach! After what seemed like a very long time, Rory dragged him onto the sand and lay down, exhausted himself now.

Jenny was weeping with relief and just held both the dogs close to her, rubbing them with a dry towel, trying to get some heat into them. Eventually, both Jack and Rory stood up, shook themselves dry, and looked at one another.

'Woof,' Jack said as he pawed Rory affectionately as if to say: 'Thank you for saving me; I know you don't really like swimming out of your depth. If you hadn't come out for me I would have drowned! I promise I'll never chase after another duck ever again.'

'Woof, woof,' replied Rory, meaning: 'As long as you've learnt your lesson; never be lured into a place you aren't familiar with.' Jack came up and nuzzled his friend affectionately. He knew he had a lucky escape and how fortunate he was to have such a brave friend.

Aside from Frankie

Me again. Sometimes, in Granny Trish's stories, you learn important lessons. Granny Trish says that's called 'the moral of the story' like in the story 'The Boy Who Cried Wolf' the moral is that we shouldn't lie, else when we finally tell the truth people might not believe us.

*What do you think the moral of **this** story is?*

Story 6:
TRAINING CLASSES

Jenny decided that, after the escapade at the beach with the ducks, it was perhaps time to take Jack and Rory for puppy training sessions. So, she made enquiries and enrolled them into a class the following week.

Her friend Laura also had a new puppy, a gorgeous black Labrador girl called Ginny, so she was enrolled too. Because it wouldn't have been possible for Jenny to control two puppies alone at the class, Finn volunteered to be with Rory, while Jenny took Jack. Off they went one Monday night to their first session in Kirkcaldy. Meeting Laura inside the hall, they were amazed to see so many different breeds of very excited puppies, tales wagging, tongues hanging out, noses in the air, little (or in some cases long) legs ready to go, go, go!

Jack, Rory, and Ginny looked around the hall, there were a few Labradors like themselves, but also a Boxer, a Dalmatian, a German Shepherd, Poodles, Westies, a Bulldog, a Dachshund, and Border Terriers. All in all, there were fifteen puppies, it was pandemonium!

Suddenly, Sonia, the dog trainer, blew her whistle and, as if by magic, the noise and chatter stopped. 'Ok, ladies and gentlemen, please form a circle and walk your puppy close to your side in a clockwise direction,' the trainer asked.

This was easier said than done. The puppies pulled on their leads, each desperate to sniff the puppy in front of them. Some of them yapped, trying to nip the legs of other owners and puppies. Some sat down and refused to move at all, and some pulled their owners so hard they nearly fell over. It was total chaos!

The trainer blew her whistle again, and silence fell. 'Well,' she said, 'now I can see why you have brought your puppies to class, but we'll have them sorted out by the end of the six sessions, by which time your puppy should be walking quietly on the lead, sitting when asked, and staying when commanded. When you receive your end-of-class certificate you should have a perfectly well-behaved puppy.'

The owners looked at one another in disbelief. Jenny and Laura burst out laughing, along with a few others.

'If that happens,' one man chirped, 'I'll eat my dog's lead!'

By the end of the second session, Rory was behaving very well, listening to Finn, and doing everything he was asked to do. Jack and Ginny, on the other hand, were being a bit silly, nudging one another, chasing their tails, pulling on their leads, and desperately trying to mingle with the other puppies. At the end of the session, the trainer asked Jenny and Laura to stay behind. When everyone else had gone, she told them in a very stern voice that the reason the puppies were not behaving was because of them. They chatted too much and didn't pay attention to instructions, so how could they expect their puppies to know what to do? If they weren't prepared to behave themselves, it might be better not to come back. Jenny and Laura left with their tails between their legs, truly mortified at being told off, but they were giggling by the time they reached Matt and Tom, Laura's husband, who had come to collect them. When they told them about getting their fingers rapped, the men decided that they would take over and go to the training sessions instead, as the women had obviously proved to be hopeless.

'Oh well,' said Jenny and Laura, slightly in a huff, 'see if you can do any better.'

For the next four classes, Jack and Ginny pulled their socks up and were as well behaved as Rory and the other puppies. The final class arrived and they were all presented with a certificate, proving that they had successfully completed the course and were capable of walking to heel, sitting, staying, and lying down when asked; they also knew how to fetch and retrieve.

'Before you go,' the trainer said, 'I have a special trophy to give out to the most improved dog of the course!'

She brought a beautiful cup out of her bag and strode across the hall, straight towards Matt.

'This is for Jack, who has excelled since you took over his training,' she said with a smile to him. (Jenny thought Sonia liked Matt a little bit too much!).

Matt was flabbergasted, but couldn't wait to gloat about Jack's achievement to Jenny, who raised her eyebrows and muttered something about Sonia trying to butter Matt up through a silly trophy. Finn was very proud of both Jack and Rory, but especially Jack, although he couldn't help wishing that he had been the one to get the trophy, as Jack was really *his* dog. Still, he thought, thank goodness Dad had taken over from Mum, otherwise, who knows what kind of silly, naughty, dog Jack would have turned out to be!

Aside from Frankie

I don't think Jenny liked Sonia the dog trainer very much, and I'm not too sure why – Granny Trish says I'll understand when I'm older. Even if Jenny wasn't keen on the trainer, she had to agree that she did a good job of helping Jack and Rory become better behaved dogs! I think the moral of this story is you should always pay attention in class and if you work hard and listen to the teacher, even the naughtiest student can improve!

Story 7:

THE STING!

When Rory was seven months old, not fully grown but quite a big boy, he was out for a walk one evening at the local park with Jack, Jenny, and Matt. It was almost the end of September, so it was still quite warm but getting chilly at night. The dogs were enjoying running around on the grass, chasing balls – and the occasional squirrel. Rory, who was always the more curious of the two dogs, ran off to investigate a smell in some nearby trees.

Suddenly, he squealed out loudly. When Matt and Jenny turned to look at what had happened, Rory was whimpering, trying to rub his head and face on the ground. Jack and Matt reached him first and were horrified to see about thirty wasps crawling all over Rory's head, stinging him repeatedly! Jenny arrived and shouted, 'Get him to the pond quickly! Hurry, he's really hurting!'

Within seconds, they managed to drag Rory to the edge of the pond, where he plunged into the water. Immediately the wasps flew off and out came Rory looking very sorry for himself indeed, poor boy.

When they arrived home, Jenny phoned the vet to explain what had happened. He told her to bathe the stings with warm, salty water and stay with Rory overnight in case he went into ana-phylactic shock (that's another way of saying he could react very badly to the stings and collapse or perhaps even die). There wasn't anything else they could do but wait and hope he would get through the night. Jenny and Matt took it in turns to soothe Rory and, to their huge relief, by the morning he was back to his old self, licking Matt and Jenny to death as if to say 'thank you for being with me, I'm fine now and I'll never go mooching around that rough grass around the trees again!'

Towards the end of summer when the nights get much cooler, wasps go into a lazy, grumpy state and what Rory had done was disturb a wasp 'bike', which homed thousands of sleepy, bad-tempered wasps. So be careful; don't go raking around, poking into things when it's getting colder – it might just be a wasp bike!

Aside from Frankie

Granny Trish always wags her finger at us when she tells that end bit to make sure we really listen. It's good advice though; I'd hate to get stung by lots of wasps! I was stung by just one and that really hurt! Poor Rory was stung by loads more so it must have been really, really bad!

Story 8:

THE HOLIDAY

Every year, the whole family left their home and went off for their summer holiday to Aviemore, where the boys had the time of their lives: swimming, sailing, running in the woods, barbecuing, building dams in the river by the holiday cottage, and generally having a great time.

The dogs also had a holiday in the kennels! This was a very new experience for them and it both confused and interested them. They were confused because they couldn't understand why the family had abandoned them, and they were interested because there were lots of new friends to be made and new walks with new smells to be had.

Because they were from the same family, Jack and Rory shared a large double kennel with a huge outside run, where they could get to know the neighbours on either side of the mesh fencing. On their first visit to the kennels, their next-door neighbours were a very large Newfoundland called Bernie and, on the other side, two Westies called Fred and Ginger.

They all got on famously and looked forward to their long walks with Maggie the kennel worker, who threw balls and shouted enthusiastically to whoever got the ball first (usually Jack, who was incredibly competitive). The others didn't mind though; they enjoyed being out in the fields running and barking at each other, rolling over, sniffing new smells, and just having fun.

One day, on the last day of their holidays, the firm friends were running through the grass when suddenly Fred yelped out in pain and rolled over onto his side. The other dogs ran to help him, along with Maggie who knelt beside the now squealing Fred.

Maggie gently rolled Fred onto his back and saw immediately what the problem was: There, at the top of his inner thigh, a large piece of glass was sticking out and his leg lay at a strange angle. Looking around, Maggie saw the remains of a fire with broken glass and food cartons scattered all over the grass. Some picnickers had left their mess behind and poor Fred had been hurt because of their carelessness!

Maggie quickly carried Fred back to the kennels, with a now very subdued line of worried dogs following her. She phoned the local vet and arranged an appointment to bring him into the surgery.

Poor Fred had to have twenty-five stitches in his leg; he was extremely brave for a wee fellow! The worst part was having to wear a plastic collar around his neck for two weeks to stop him from licking the wound and infecting the stitches.

Aside from Frankie

Please remember if you are going for a picnic or a barbecue in the countryside or at the seaside you should always, always take your rubbish home with you – especially any glass – that way you can keep everyone safe! Granny Trish also says that we should never litter because it not only looks bad and could hurt someone, it's also bad for the environment. If everyone does their bit we can make the world a much better place!

Story 9:

THE FENCE

Some time later, on a lovely sunny morning, Jenny set off with the dogs on a walk. She decided to take them on one of their favourite walks which was out of town. It had everything they loved: grass, woods, hills to run up, fences to jump over, rabbits to chase, small ponds to cool off in, and friends to meet up with. When they got to the location, there were no other cars in the car park, so they walked off on their own. Because it was such a lovely day, Jenny decided they would go right up the hill and pass by the pond where the dogs could have a quick drink.

Sometimes the cattle from a nearby farm came down from their field to have a nosey at the humans and dogs, so the farmer had put up a low fence and stile to keep the cattle out of the main path area, but, if you crossed the fence to carry on up the steep hill, the cows generally didn't worry and you could continue without any fuss.

On either side of the path, fruit trees and bushes had been planted and now their branches were full of apples, cherries, raspberries, and there were even some wild strawberries! Jenny stopped to pick some ripe cherries and raspberries. Jack, who couldn't resist grabbing some rasps as well, licked his lips and trotted after Jenny and Rory.

As she approached the stile, Jenny looked around and thought, *there is something different,* but she couldn't quite work out what it was. With Rory beside her, they waited for Jack to catch up so they could start up the hill – *ah, there he was trotting along.* He raced towards them, jumped over the fence, and stood wagging his tail, looking up at Jenny.

But she was laughing so hard that tears were running down her rosy cheeks!

She walked back over the stile, Rory was now by her side. *How odd,* thought Jack, *I'm sure Jenny said we were going right up the hill for the long walk.* He jumped over the fence to sit by Jenny again, noticing that she was laughing more than ever.

'Oh Jack, you are a silly boy,' she giggled.

Jack was a bit miffed. Why did she think he was silly and not Rory? Then Jenny pointed to the fence and Jack understood why she was so amused: There was no fence anymore, only the stile.

Someone had taken the fence down and he had imagined that it was still there in his mind so he had jumped over thin air! No wonder they both thought he was silly. However, he decided that, to make a point, whenever he came on this walk he would continue to jump over thin air, just to make everyone laugh.

When the family were all sitting around the supper table that evening, Jenny told them the story of Jack's invisible fence and they all laughed at the picture she painted. Finn reached out to Jack and ruffled his head. 'Never mind, Jack. It will always be your fence, whether it's there or not,' he said.

From then on, whenever the family went for a walk there, they always stopped to watch Jack jump over his invisible fence.

And he never let them down!

Aside from Frankie

Granny Trish says there isn't a moral to that story, it's just a nice funny one. But I disagree, I think the moral of the story is that you should always have fun, and don't get embarrassed if you do something a bit silly. It might make people happy!

I just told Granny Trish my idea about the moral of the story and she said, 'Aye, pet. I think you might be right!'

Story 10:

LOST BOY

Matt and Jenny were going to their friends Laura and Tom's house for supper. When they did supper with friends, everyone usually took some food so the host didn't have to do all the work.

Jenny popped up to her friend with her 'course' for the night, and then she planned to take the dogs for a walk. Matt had gone sailing with three of the boys and would be back in time to join everyone for supper.

When Jenny arrived at the house, Tom was heading out with his dogs for a walk and offered to take Jack and Rory with him. Jenny wasn't sure if that was a good idea as Jack could some-times be a bit funny when someone else took him out, but Tom insisted, 'Oh, he'll be fine,' so Jenny agreed, and off they all went. Jenny had a quick coffee with Laura and left for home as Tom had said he would drop the dogs back after their walk. She was hardly in the front door when the phone rang, it was Tom asking if Jack was with her!

'What do you mean is Jack with me? You took all the dogs for a walk!' Jenny exclaimed.

'Erm, yes,' said Tom, 'but he ran away and I couldn't find him so I thought perhaps he had run home.'

Considering Jack had never been to the park Tom had taken them to and it was four miles from his home, Jenny thought it highly unlikely that Jack would know where he was… now she was really worried!

Jenny dropped what she was doing, rushed to the car, and returned to Laura and Tom's house. They all went down to the park shouting Jack's name and retracing the route Tom had taken with the dogs.

But no luck; there was no Jack, no sign of him at all. Jenny was frantic, Jack was a very handsome dog and she was very worried that he had been stolen. She tried phoning Matt on his mobile, but he didn't answer, so she left a message and decided to come home with Rory and wait for Matt to get home. After what seemed like days, Matt appeared, looking as worried as Jenny. They agreed that the best plan of action was to return to the park and keep looking. If they were whistling and shouting for

Jack, he had to hear them eventually. Their friends came with them, but after a few hours, when Jack had not appeared, they decided to leave the search as it was now dark. Matt phoned the police, the dog warden, and the vet to make sure no one had found Jack and handed him over, but again, no luck. Matt and Jenny were very concerned now, where could he be? They decided to try once more before they went to bed, and looked at all the places Jack was normally taken for a walk, but nothing; there was no sign of him anywhere.

They came back home despondent, and tried to get some sleep but couldn't, so by 5 a.m. they were both up, dressed, and ready to continue with the search for their lost dog. They revisited all the familiar walks the dogs had been on, but still found nothing. Then Jenny said, 'Look Matt, I think we should split up and cover more places. It will mean we are doubling the search area.'

Matt agreed, and they set off in different directions. Jenny decided to start back at the park where Jack had first gone missing. It had been more than twelve hours since he had disappeared; he would be so frightened, cold, and hungry.

She was driving uphill to the park when she spotted a man walking down with his two dogs from a very early walk. On a hunch, she stopped the car, wound the window down, and asked the man if by any chance he had seen a black Labrador running on his own. 'Yes, as a matter of fact, I have,' he said, 'I saw a dog running back and forth looking very lost but when I tried to encourage him to come to me, he just backed away and I couldn't get hold of him.'

Jenny gratefully thanked him and set off for the park. She knew in her heart it was Jack and raced to get there as quickly as she could. Drawing into the car park she noticed the park attendant picking up the litter. Getting out of the car she shouted across to him, 'You haven't seen a black lab on his own, have you? I lost my dog here yesterday,' but before the 'parkie' could reply, Jenny impulsively turned, and there in the distance was a black Labrador limping towards her. It was Jack!

Jenny ran towards him, tears streaming down her cheeks. Jack saw her and broke into a run, it was just like a scene from a film.

They both ran together and Jack jumped up, putting his front paws on Jenny's shoulders, licking her face over and over, with Jenny calling his name again and again. The parkie was emotional, too, and said he was so glad Jenny had found Jack. He said he had a dog himself and couldn't imagine how awful it would be to lose him.

Jenny quickly put Jack into the car and drove home, just pausing briefly to phone Matt and give him the good news.

When he arrived back home in the kitchen, Jack collapsed on the floor. Matt examined his paws and was horrified to see the state they were in. They were raw and bleeding, he must have run backwards and forwards frantically not knowing where he was; alone, lost, and frightened all night long! Poor, poor boy.

Matt and Jenny bathed his feet, bandaging them securely. Meanwhile, Rory lay down beside Jack, licking his face and nudging him gently as if to say, *you're safe now my friend, we're all here for you. We missed you so much, but you're home now; close your eyes and rest.* It took three or four days before Jack could walk even a few steps, but eventually, he recovered enough to go for a short walk, and soon he was back to normal, running and playing with Rory – but always checking that either Matt or Jenny were close by.

He never went for a walk without a family member again.

Story 11:

FOR THE LOVE OF RORY

The years rolled by and the boys all grew up, each leaving home for university, the army, and Australia. Which only left Finn to keep Matt, Jenny, and the dogs in order.

The dogs still enjoyed their walks and being with each other. Plus, they were all in good health. However, on one of their annual visits to the vet, Jack sailed through his check-up but it was discovered that Rory had a slight problem with his heart and needed a wee operation to sort it out.

'It's nothing serious,' the vet said, 'we can sort the valve out and he won't even have to stay overnight.'

Everyone was relieved at that thought and, the following week, Jenny drove Rory to the vet's for his small procedure. Jenny didn't know the vet who came forward when they arrived; previously, they had always had the same vet looking after the dogs. The new vet introduced herself and led Jenny and Rory into the consulting room.

The vet explained what would happen when they took Rory through to the operating theatre, reassuring Jenny that it was a normal operation and wouldn't take too long. She laughingly joked that she hoped she could concentrate on the operation as she was very excited. This was her last day at the practice, and the next day she was setting off for a year's trekking in India.

I hope you can concentrate! thought Jenny. *This is my precious dog you are operating on*. However, she had many things to do and left Rory in the safe hands of the vet.

Just as Finn arrived home from school, the phone rang. It was the vet to say Rory was in recovery and could be collected in thirty minutes. All had gone according to plan and he should be up wagging his tail in a few hours, and running around with his pal Jack again in a couple of days.

Jenny was very relieved. She and Finn set off for the vet's clinic, eager to bring Rory home. When they arrived at the practice, the vet brought Rory out to them. He seemed a bit sleepy and wobbly on his feet but he was very pleased to see his family and licked them both, wagging his tail nineteen to the dozen. They set off for home where Jack and Matt were waiting and Rory lay down in his bed. He was fast asleep almost before his head even hit his blanket. After an hour's rest, he got up and wandered over to his water dish for a long drink – anaesthetic can make dogs very thirsty, you know.

It was a warm autumn day; Rory was panting quite a bit so they let him wander out to the garden, where he flopped down and fell asleep again. Matt always sailed his boat on a Wednesday evening, so after checking on Rory, he left to pick up his friend who went sailing with him.

Finn had been playing football with friends at the local park and Jenny was baking a cake for him as it was his sixteenth birthday the next day.

Suddenly, Finn rushed into the kitchen shouting,

'Mum! Mum! Something is wrong with Rory, please come outside!'

Jenny rushed outside and could see immediately that Rory was not well at all: he was panting, his tongue had flopped out, and his gums were white. He had wee'd just where he lay and was obviously not able to get up. Finn was a tall, strong boy by now and he managed to pick Rory up and put him onto the back seat of the car before jumping into the passenger seat.

Jenny raced to the vet's clinic, her heart pounding. This time, when they arrived their usual vet came out to help Finn bring Rory into the consulting room. Quickly he and his nurse assistant examined Rory, hooking him up to a drip and covering him with a heated blanket. The vet looked up at Jenny and Finn and explained that Rory had gone into shock but they didn't know why yet; they would find out as quickly as possible and do everything they could to save him.

Jenny and Finn sat nervously in the waiting room supporting each other. The vet appeared and told them that there was a small tear in Rory's artery, which had probably happened when he had been stitched after his op. They had fixed the tear but they would keep him under observation, as he was still a very sick doggie and the next twelve hours would be crucial if he was to survive.

Jenny and Finn were stunned, they went home to tell Matt what had happened. When they walked into the house they all just hugged and wept. The family adored and loved their dogs so much, the thought of Rory being so ill and the fact they could do nothing to help him was devastating for them.

The vet had told them he would phone to let them know how Rory was doing later that evening and when the phone rang they all jumped. Matt answered, he listened carefully then quietly put the phone down looking very glum. The vet had told him that Rory was still very poorly, but he had warmed up and the drip seemed to be helping his condition. He said he would call again in a few hours to give them an update.

No one said anything for a while, then suddenly Finn looked up having had an idea. 'We all have to concentrate and send our love through to Rory,' he reasoned, 'he'll know how much we love and care about him and that will help him.'

So that is exactly what they did. Holding each other, they sent their love and prayed that their beloved dog would make it through the night. Jack lay at their feet; he knew there was something wrong. Where was his friend, what had happened to him?

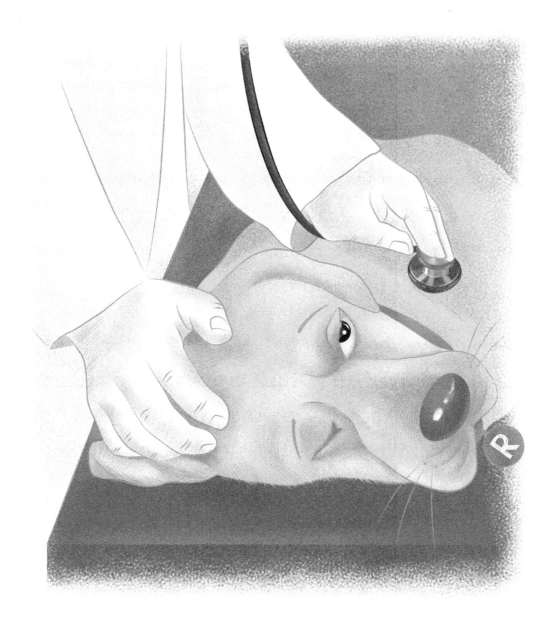

After four very long hours, the vet rang again. When Matt put the phone down he looked at Jenny and Finn and said, with a relieved smile, 'He's going to be ok. He's off the drip, his gums are back to normal colour, and he is sleeping peacefully.'

They were all grinning now and Jack was jumping up licking everyone, not really knowing what was going on but realising that the mood had changed and his people were happy. Rory stayed in the animal ward for another night, just to make sure he was 100% fit enough to return home. The next day, they all went to collect him, even Jack. When they got home, Rory thought he was in seventh heaven as he was pampered, cuddled, stroked, and given the most delicious treats.

Soon he was able to go for walks with his mate Jack, and enjoy his life once more. The family had gone through a horrible experience but realised that, for the love of Rory, he had survived and was back with them. They would all be wiser, better people in the knowledge that love can work miracles.

Aside from Frankie

Poor Rory. He was very unlucky to have had something go wrong in his operation but very lucky to have been ok! Granny Trish tells me that I shouldn't worry if I ever need to have an operation, or if anyone I love does either, because there is only a really, really small chance of anything going wrong like this.

Story 12:

JACK AND DOMINO

Because it was just Jenny and Matt in the family home now (Finn had left to go to university in Edinburgh), it was obvious that it was too big for them, so they decided to move to a smaller house by the coast. This meant different walks for Jack and Rory, with new smells and coastal paths to negotiate. Plus, lots of new doggy friends to introduce themselves to. They loved this new adventure in their lives.

Everyone settled into the new house, even Domino, the family's ancient cat. Despite a horrible accident when she was very young, she had survived and patrolled her domain totally without fear of the dogs. She wasn't even afraid of the two Labradors who were in the family before Jack and Rory. Such was her confidence that she ruled the roost.

When Jenny and Matt moved house, Domino was already twenty – a bit creaky but still fairly active. When they had lived in the big house there was loads of room inside, however, it had a small back garden with no grass, just a patio area. Moving to the new house had lots of advantages for everyone, not least Domino, who thrived on the fact that there was a large back garden and GRASS! She *loved* the grass and felt she had been given a new lease of life with the move. She certainly looked younger and happier.

She paraded around the garden at her leisure, throwing angry looks at the dogs if they dared to run around in what she had now decided was *her* garden.

Rory was always the quieter of the two dogs and he just let her get on with life. But Jack was a different kettle of fish; he totally regarded himself as the boss and took offence at this little black-and-white cat giving him orders. Who did she think she was, growling at him and Rory if they dared to play catch and run in the garden, or come close to her little 'cat house' on the decking.

Every morning when Jack came downstairs Domino would glare at him, then stretch, yawn, and glare at him some more. Every morning Jack would glare back and then rush across the kitchen to menace her.

Every morning Domino would arch her back when she saw Jack coming towards her, hiss, and lash out at his nose when he came too close. Some days she even managed to make contact with his nose and Jack would yelp in pain and scurry off to nurse his nose and his wounded pride.

It was a ritual that went on for years. They were never going to call a truce, each one hoping for the day that the other one wasn't there.

They had been in their new house for almost four years. It was winter and a very cold one, but Domino, now twenty-four, still loved roaming around the garden and making sure, in her mind that she was in charge – not that big, black, silly dog. Humph!

Jenny had made a very cosy 'cat house' for Domino, where she could cuddle in and keep warm when she didn't want to come into the house. It was on the decking and kept the wind and rain out, so Domino always had somewhere safe and secure to go to when she felt like staying out all night to meet up with her other cat friends.

On a particularly freezing cold night that winter, Jenny called Domino to come into the warmth. She shouted repeatedly, but Domino didn't appear. When they were ready to go upstairs to bed, Jenny called on Domino once more but there was still no sign of her. She decided to put a hot water bottle in the little cat house. *That way at least she'll be warm even if she hasn't come inside*, she thought as she went off to bed.

The next morning, Jack came downstairs first, sniffing about for 'that cat'. Maybe this time he would manage to lash back at her.

Funny, he thought. She was usually sitting preening herself in her bed but there was no sign of her. *Oh well, I'll get her later,* and off he went with Matt and Rory for their morning walk.

Jenny was next to come downstairs, opening the patio door, she stepped out onto the decking calling for Domino. *Brrrr,* she thought, *it's perishing. Come on pussy where are you? Come and get your breakfast.* Suddenly, she was aware of something lying on the decking, near the cat house, not moving. *Oh no!* – it was Domino.

It had been so windy during the night, the door to Domino's little refuge had jammed shut and the poor little thing hadn't been able to push it open. She had been so cold that she had just fallen asleep and never woke up. Jenny felt so guilty; if only she had persevered calling on Domino, she would be safe and warm now.

Matt arrived back with the dogs and immediately saw that Jenny was upset about something. When she told him what had happened, he put his arms around her, saying, 'Look, it wasn't your fault. You tried, you even left her cat house nice and cosy, with a hotty. Tragically, the wind blew the door shut but it wasn't your fault. She had a very happy, long life with us and it was her time to go.' Jack was sniffing around the decking searching for Domino. He looked up and saw her in Jenny's arms, *what was wrong? She wasn't hissing at him, in fact, she wasn't moving at all.* Rory nudged Jack softly and looked at him as if to say, *I think something has happened to Domino, I think she's passed away.*

Jack couldn't believe it, no more hissing, no more trying to avoid the nose scratching every day, no more chasing her around the garden. No more Domino. He suddenly realised he would miss her and felt bad that he had sometimes thought life would be better if she wasn't around.

Oh dear, he thought, *be careful what you wish for*!

Aside from Frankie

Poor Jack must have felt really bad that he wasn't nicer to Domino, but I don't think Domino minded too much – by the sounds of it she enjoyed their rivalry! It's sad that Domino passed away but Granny Trish says that she was really, really old and had a lovely life so we shouldn't be too sad.

Story 13:

HOLIDAYS WITH FRIENDS

Twice a year, Jenny and Matt went on holiday with their friends, Laura and Tom, and all of the dogs. They would go to a beautiful cottage on the Black Isle, near Inverness.

The cottage was on the banks of Munlochy Bay and everyone, including the dogs, loved the peace and quiet, the walks, the countryside smells (especially the dogs), the sea life, and generally relaxing with friends.

Because the cottage was surrounded by trees and out of the wind it was usually warm and they could barbecue and eat outdoors. Beside the cottage was a huge quarry which wasn't in use now, and lots of trees and bushes had taken over the rocky sides of the quarry. This was now a perfect home for a herd of cashmere goats, who ran up and down munching the grassy slopes and nudging their noses through the fence. They watched the dogs and the friends in the hope of getting something tastier than grass and roots. The smells from the barbecue were very tantalising and goats are always curious.

The herd belonged to Colin and Jane who lived in the neighbouring cottage. Jane collected the cashmere hair from the goats and turned it into socks, hats, and scarves; quite a little cottage industry, which in turn gave them extra cash.

Sadly, over the years, one by one, the goats passed away until the twins Barry and Larry were the only two left. By then they were too old to produce decent cashmere, and Jane herself was unwell and wasn't able to collect the cashmere and make the goodies, so the twins had a very leisurely life and were always very friendly with Jenny and co. Sometimes they would even jump the fence in search of some titbits and a stroke. They missed the company of the other goats and were glad to see the return of the dogs and humans.

One late April morning, they all woke up to a snowy scene. Snow had fallen all night and it was very deep. The weight of the snow on the electricity lines had brought many electric poles down so now there was no heat, lighting, or hot water.

'Ooooh,' said Jenny, 'what are we going to do, we can't possibly get up the hill. The snow is so deep, the cars just won't manage to get through.'

The dogs ran outside, rolling around in the snow, snuffling it up in the air, and having a great time. If dogs could laugh out loud they were definitely all chuckling!

However, that didn't solve their problem of being stuck with no heating or light. They had plenty of food to last for a few days and there were farms nearby who had tractors to clear the lanes eventually, but for now, they would have to improvise!

Next to the cottage was a barn that was home to the goats in winter. The barn also stored an enormous amount of logs, a barbecue, and a pizza oven, so they would be able to keep warm in the cottage with the wood-burning fire and they could use the barbecue and pizza oven to make meals. They had torches and candles, so life wasn't too bad and actually, it looked very pretty outside with everything covered in snow.

In the afternoon, they ventured up and over the hill with the dogs and hiked through the snow down to the water's edge.

The dogs decided that trailing along in the snow was cold enough, so having a swim was not an option that day – they would leave swimming with the seals for another time.

On their return, Matt, Tom, and the dogs went out to the barn to light the barbecue.

When the food was almost ready Jenny and Laura came out with travel rugs, the dogs' food, marshmallows, chocolate, bananas, a mixture to make mulled wine, and the wine of course!

As they all sat around the warmth of the barbecue on straw bales, they decided it hadn't been too bad a day, all things considered. While they had been chomping down the burgers, sausages, and baked potatoes, Jenny had wrapped the bananas, chocolate, and marshmallows in tin foil and put them on the barbecue.

Now they were ready to eat, and the four friends *mmmmmmm'd* their way through the delicious pudding. No chocolate for the dogs, of course, as it is poisonous to them, but they got lots of savoury, tasty titbits from the barbecue. After clearing everything away they all went off to bed, watching the stars in the clear sky and hoping there would be no more snow.

The next morning Jenny woke up to even *more* snow! She went into the kitchen to make tea and realised that was impossible as there was still no electricity. By now everyone was up, and the men trotted out to the barn to put the barbecue on again. After a warm breakfast of bacon, eggs, toast, and tea, Matt, Tom, and the dogs went out for their morning walk. The dogs ran about enjoying the snow, which was almost up to their tummies, and thought that, even though it was cold, it sure was fun!

When they returned, Jenny and Laura were grinning at them from the cottage door,

'The electricity has been turned back on!' they shouted, 'we have light and heat – yippee!'

Laughing, the men shook off their coats and sat down beside the fire to heat up and munch on warm scones and tea. The dogs were kindly given sneaky pieces of tasty scone, too.

The snow disappeared almost as soon as it had fallen, and for the rest of that holiday, the weather was sunny and warm. What a funny climate we have, they all agreed: snow, sun, frost, and barbecues all in one week! You can never predict what might happen with the weather in Scotland.

Aside from Frankie

My mum always wants to go somewhere hot for our holidays, but I think this snowy one sounds super fun! I'd be able to drink lots of hot chocolate and make snowmen! What kind of holiday do you like?

Story 14:

OUR LOVELY LIVES

Jack and Rory had been with the family for more than thirteen years now. They had brought love, loyalty, fun, and joy to everyone and the family had loved each and every day they spent with them.

Dogs don't usually have a long lifespan; it varies between ten and fifteen years, depending on the breed and size of the dog, and how healthy they are.

Both Jack and Rory had been very lucky to have had healthy lives but their time to go was near. Within six months of each other, they had both passed away. Jack peacefully went first and then Rory followed his friend not long after.

Matt, Jenny, and Finn were devastated by the loss of their doggy friends, but they also had wonderful memories of the happy years they had spent together and they often laughed when they remembered the funny adventures they had.

Even at the very end of his life, Rory had made them chuckle because, for some reason known only to himself, he would only drink out of puddles, and it became quite hard to find puddles if there had been no rain.

They had both given and received so much love. The family could only be glad that they had been so lucky to have them in their lives for such a long time. They would always remember their dogs with huge amounts of love and affection.

EPILOGUE

I always feel a bit sad when Granny Trish talks about Jack and Rory going to doggie heaven, but at least they had each other. Granny Trish says we don't know what happens when we pass on but she thinks that Jack and Rory are somewhere really nice having adventures together with Domino and all of their favourite things.

I hope you enjoyed The Stories of Jack and Rory as much as I do, and that the end didn't upset you too much. Granny Trish always says I should have a go at writing down my own stories about pets (or anything I want) and that always cheers me up. So, I'll leave some space for you to write your own story on the next page. Just in case…

Love,

Frankie x

Made in the USA
Monee, IL
24 July 2022

10254686R00044